Square in a Square™

Jodi Barrows

Quiltingly Yours
Jodi Barrows

2116 Nevada
Liberal, Kansas 67901
(316) 624-6260 • FAX (316) 624-3115
Toll Free 1-888-624-6260
email qyjodi@aol.com
web www.quiltinglyyours.com

Square in a Square™

2116 Nevada
Liberal, Kansas 67901
(316) 624-6260 • FAX (316) 624-3115
Toll Free 1-888-624-6260
email qyjodi@aol.com
web www.quiltinglyyours.com

ISBN: 1-885156-17-0

Printed on Recycled Paper

CREDITS:

Editor	Kim Gjere
Graphics	Jackie Robinson
Photography	Christopher Marona

Meet Jodi Barrows

Jodi was born and raised in Southwest Kansas. She and her husband, Steve, have two sons, Nick and Tucker. An avid quilter since 1986, she's received several honors including the Five State Fair's Viewers Choice award and having a quilt hang in the National Quilt Museum in Ellicott City, Maryland. Jodi is one of 15 quilters chosen for the Kansas Historical Society Exhibit, "What Mother Did, I Did Too".

She enjoys teaching classes, giving trunk shows from her collection of more than 200 quilts, and judging shows and fairs.

Dedication

I dedicate this book to all of my family for nurturing my talent.

Acknowledgements

Thank you so very much to my Aunt Elaine and my husband Steve for their computer time, and to my niece Scarlette for her excellent proof reading. You guys are a Whizz!

Special thanks to the quilters who helped me quilt these quilts: Mary Lou Alexander, Sarah Amish, Maryanne Cammarata, Linda Colvin, Anita Dunn, Marva Herald, Dianna Matthews, Martha Vainridge, Centerville Iowa Baptist Quilters, and the Forgan, OK. Golden Agers.

The Quilts:

Order the Square in A Square™ ruler from:

Quiltingly Yours
2116 Nevada
Liberal, KS 67901
(316) 624-6260

$ 19.95 + $4.95 shipping

Cover Photos:
Front: **Prairie Claw**, 89" x 100"
Back: **Disappearing Star**, 54" x 72"

Supplies

Rotary Equipment

All the quilts were cut using rotary cutting tools. Always have a sharp blade in your cutter and a nice size mat. Serious quilters should consider having several sizes of self healing mats. Large pieces of fabric need a large mat; scraps can be cut on a smaller mat.

Use an accurate rotary ruler with clear measurements, including 1/8" marks. You will need a Square in a Square™ (SnS) ruler or a ruler with 30°, 45°, and 60° lines. The SnS ruler was developed specifically for these quilts and makes cutting angles a breeze. See page 3 for ordering.

Sewing Machine

Use a clean, oiled sewing machine with a size 70 or 80 needle. Make sure the tension is adjusted to produce a smooth seam.

Iron

A heavy, hot, steam iron will improve the quality of your work. Keep it close to your machine, for frequent pressing is a basic. A good rule to remember is to press to the dark or to the largest area without seams.

Fabric

Use 100% cotton, quality fabric. Yardage given is actual, plus 10% for shrinkage and small cutting errors.

You know you are a fabric collector if you spend time playing and organizing your collection. I am also a fabric user, I use it up and even throw it out on occasion.

Since I don't always have a project in mind when purchasing fabric, I buy varying amounts. I like quilts with a variety of fabric. They are more appealing and interesting to me. Therefore, I use a lot of fat quarters. They provide a good mix of fabric and shorter strips when rotary cutting. Also, when you use many fabrics you are not backed into a corner if you run short; just add another choice. If a fabric would make a good border, buy 2-1/2 yards. Buy 3-1/2 yards for a background. If a fabric really appeals to me I get 1-2 yards. If only two or three fabrics are used, you will need larger cuts. I don't prewash fabric, repeat, I don't prewash. I find piecing is more accurate with sizing in the fabric. If I'm concerned about it running, I test it and treat as necessary.

Batting

There are many choices in batting. I have used most of them and like cotton the best. It gives the quilts an antique look. Pretreat the batting as suggested on the package.

General Directions

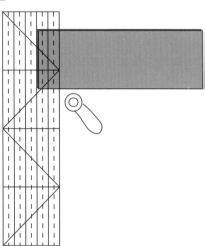

Cutting

You will be cutting strips of fabric from yardage or fat quarters. Cutting instructions are given for full widths, 42" - 44". If using fat quarters, simply cut twice as many strips as stated. Fold or layer the fabric. Make a clean up cut on one edge. You can cut about six layers at once. More than that is risky, as the fabric shifts.

Often the directions call for crosscuts. These are made on strips or strip sets (strips sewn together).

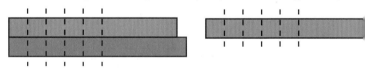

Machine Piecing

Machine piecing is strong, fast and accurate. Learn to sew a 1/4" seam; it is a must. To test your 1/4" seam, stitch together three 1-1/2" x 6" strips along the 6" edge. Press. The unit will measure 3-1/2" x 6" if the seam allowance is accurate. If it doesn't, practice until it does.

3-1/2"

For more accurate piecing, try using spray starch on the fabric before sewing. This is very helpful with miniatures.

When you have two pieces that should fit together, but don't, you will have to ease them. Pin them well and make them fit so seams and points will match up. The fullest piece should feed through the machine on the bottom. The feed dogs will help ease the fullness more evenly and the foot on top will slightly stretch the top layer.

Chain piecing has always been a natural for me. I did it before I knew someone else had invented it! Keep sewing the units, one after the other, into the machine without lifting the presser foot or cutting threads. When you change to another part of the pattern, or you have about a mile of pieces on the back of your machine, stop and cut them apart, or have the kids help to snip them. I also use a runner, which is a small scrap of fabric. I run it into the machine when I don't have a pattern piece to sew or I need to stop on the chain piecing. It just leaves the machine in neutral, ready to sew. With a runner and chain piecing, you don't have a mess with clipping all of those loose threads.

Square in a Square™

All of the quilts in this book are based on my Square in a Square™ (SnS) piecing technique. This method creates squares within each other by sewing strips and squares together. It results in extra clean cuts and accuracy not found with other methods. There are several options to the technique, you will be amazed at how versatile the SnS technique can be.

Basic Steps for Square in a Square™

All of the quilts included give detailed cutting instructions. If you want to design your own quilt, the directions which follow give formulas for calculating measurements. Round to the nearest 1/8". Use the chart below to convert the decimals on the calculator to fractions.

$$1/8 = .125$$
$$1/4 = .25$$
$$3/8 = .375$$
$$1/2 = .5$$
$$5/8 = .625$$
$$3/4 = .75$$
$$7/8 = .875$$

Since there is rounding involved in this technique the following will help you to be most accurate.

When sewing a bias and straight grain edge together, always ease or stretch the bias piece to fit the straight grain piece. Also, whenever possible, sew with straight grain edges on top and bias on the bottom.

1. Cut center square.

2. Cut corner strip the 45" width of the fabric. The width of the corner strip is half the width of the cut square, plus 1/4" [corner strip = (cut square ÷ 2) +1/4"].

3. Lay the corner strip face up on the sewing machine. Place the square face down on the strip with edges even. Sew 1/4" along the edge of square. Lay the next square down on the strip and continue on in the chain piecing method.

Repeat for the opposite side of the square.

4. Cut the squares apart and press seams out.

5. Sew strips to the other two sides of the squares. Put the square unit with the two side strips face up on the sewing machine. Lay the strip on the square, making sure the corner strip is straight on the square.

Repeat for the last side.

6. Cut the squares apart and press open, seams out.

7. Cut an SnS block. The Square in a Square™ ruler makes this step easy. Match the corner on the inside square with the corresponding angle on the ruler. A regular rotary ruler with angle lines can also be used. Trim all four corners according to the option you choose below. Notice that the corners are blunted just a little. This won't affect the finished square at all.

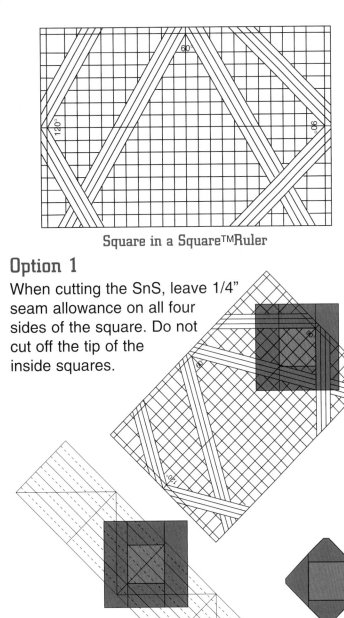

Square in a Square™Ruler

Option 1

When cutting the SnS, leave 1/4" seam allowance on all four sides of the square. Do not cut off the tip of the inside squares.

Option 2

Continue to add strips to enlarge the SnS. Refer to the math formula, Step 2, page 5, to find the width to cut the strips. The cut square is the SnS you are adding on to. Leave 1/4" seam allowances like Option 1 when cutting the SnS.

Option 3

A half SnS block is used in several of the quilts. To make these units so that two of them sewn together are the same size as one SnS block, cut the center square 3/8" larger than the center square in the full SnS block. Determine the width of the corner strips using the formula in Step 2, page 5, based on the size of the center square in the full SnS block. For example: The full SnS block uses a cut square of 2-1/2" and corner strips 1-1/2" wide. The half units are made with a 2-7/8" cut square (2-1/2" + 3/8") and corner strips 1-1/2" wide.

For this option, the block is trimmed differently. Cut two, opposite, sides of the block the same as Option 1, leaving 1/4" seam allowance. Next trim the other two sides up to the point.

Cut the SnS in half as shown.

Option 4

The SnS squares can be cut to make half square triangles. There are two formulas for making the half square triangles. If you want half square triangles so that four of them sewn together make a unit the size of an SnS, cut the center square 3/4" larger than the center square of the full SnS. Cut the corner strips half the width of the center square. For example: The full square uses a cut square of 2-1/2" and corner strips 1-1/2" wide. The half square triangles are made with a 3-1/4" square (2-1/2" + 3/4") and corner strips of 1-5/8" (3-1/4" ÷ 2).

If you just want half square triangles and they don't have to match up with a full SnS, use the following formula. Multiply the desired cut size of the half square triangle by 1.414 and add 1/2" to get the size of the center square. Round to the nearest 1/8". The corner strips are half the width of the center square. For example: You want 3" half square triangles (finished size 2-1/2"). The center square is cut 4-3/4" or [(3" x 1.414) + 1/2"]. The corner strips are cut 2-3/8" (4-3/4" ÷ 2).

Cut all four sides up to the points of the center square. Cut the square into quarters.

Option 5

Use any pattern in place of the center square.

Option 6

The pattern may call for only one, two, or three sides of the square to have corner strips sewn on. Trimming of the corner strips could be any of the Options 1, 3, or 4.

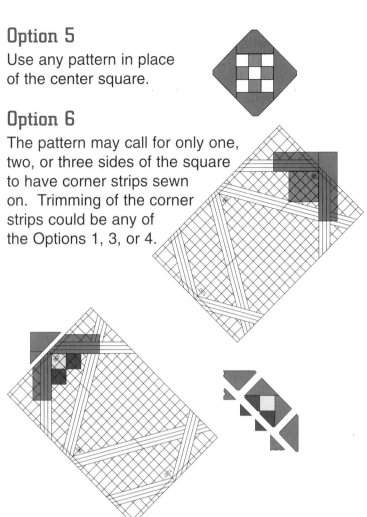

Option 7

Substitute a 60° diamond for the center square. Cut the diamonds from a strip of fabric. Lay the 60° angle on a ruler along the horizontal edge of the strip. Trim the strip along the edge of the ruler. Cut segments the same width as the strip. Check the angle every 3-4 cuts to make sure it is still 60°, recutting if necessary.

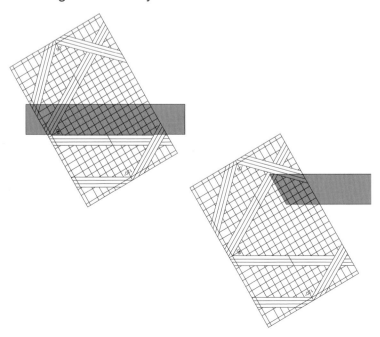

Add corner strips. Use the same formula for finding the width of the corner strips as used for squares (width of diamond strip ÷ 2 + 1/4"). Sew strips to two opposite sides first. Trim even with the diamond.

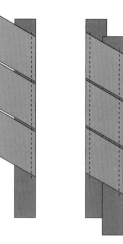

Sew corner strips to the remaining two sides. Trim.

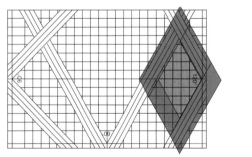

Diamond SnS are cut like either Options 1 or 3 in this book. Remember that Option 1 leaves 1/4" seam allowances on all four corners.

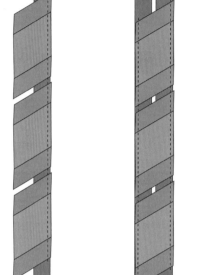

Cutting Option 3 is slightly different for a diamond than for a square center. Leave 1/4" at the sharp (60°) points of the diamond. Leave 1/8" at the other (120°) points. This is necessary to get good star points.

1/4"
1/8"   1/8"
1/4"

If using an SnS ruler, simply match the corner of the diamond to the angles on the ruler, leaving the seam allowance necessary.

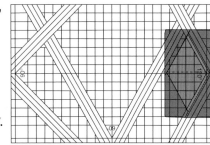

The easiest way to use a regular ruler is to have the edge of ruler 1/4" or 1/8" from the point as required by the option. Then place a line on the ruler so it is exactly on opposite points of the diamond. Trim the edge. Repeat for the other three sides, leaving the correct seam allowance.

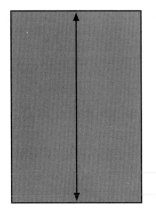

Cut the diamond in half as shown.

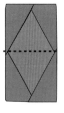

Borders

To find the correct border length, measure the center of the quilt from raw edge to raw edge. Cut two side borders this length and sew on. Repeat for the width, measurement includes the side borders. Measuring along the outside edges can cause the border to ripple. You may have to ease the border to fit. If so, put the fullness on the bottom when you sew it.

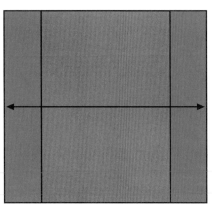

How to Check for Square Corners

Lay the quilt out flat. Do the corners have a true 90° edge when measured with a ruler? You may trim up to 1/4" without affecting the borders. More than that can cause odd border shapes and are noticeable to the eye.

Finishing

Cut the batting and backing 4" longer and wider than the quilt top. Layer all together and baste. Use large hand stitches if hand quilting and 1" safety pins if machine quilting.

Quilting is fun and time consuming. It can add a lot of character to the quilt. Heavy quilting is always admired. Plan your quilting to enhance the quilt. Make hand stitches even and as small as you can.

Machine quilting techniques have improved greatly. A walking foot is a must for straight line quilting and binding. A darning foot and dropping the feed dogs will allow you to free motion most any design. It is a lot of fun, so keep trying. Small and medium quilts are the easiest to maneuver on the sewing machine. Use cotton thread in the bobbin. Try nylon .004 in the top of the machine and adjust the top tension. For best results, use a backing fabric with a design.

Binding

Binding finishes the quilt. It makes a double layer around the edges of the quilt, keeping all three layers inside it. Cut the bindings from 2" wide for small quilts to 3" for large. Press in half lengthwise and apply binding using your favorite method. Yardage is based on 3" wide binding, wider bindings require more fabric.

Fabric Dye

For an older muted look, over dye the quilt. Dilute one box of ecru or tan color dye in a cup of warm/hot water. Add it to a full washer of warm water. Mix or agitate it for a moment or two on delicate or short cycle, cool rinse. Add your quilt, walk away and don't worry! Ha! I stand right by my washer. Stretch it out to dry. In the daily Kansas 20 MPH wind, it only takes about 20 minutes to dry. I put a sheet over the hammock and lay the quilt on that. Don't let it fade by forgetting it out in the sun, or let a bird fly over. I need a sitter, so our 15 lb. cat, Samson, lies in the middle for a cool nap and the birds stay away.

Constellation

25" x 25"
Beginner
Photograph, page 24

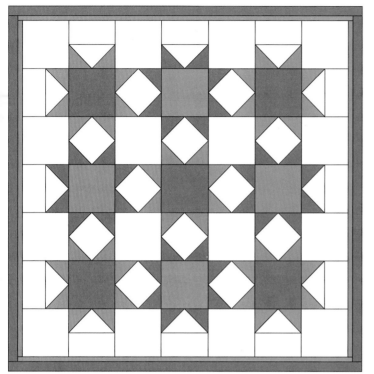

The fourth of July is always a big day at my mother's house; with family, friends and neighbors gathering. A quilt commemorating this special day was a must, out of patriotic fabric and a star pattern. I made the quilt and gave it to Mother for Christmas several years ago.

Yardage

1/2 yd.   Red
1/2 yd.   Navy
3/8 yd.   Background
1/3 yd.   Binding
7/8 yd.   Backing

Cutting

Navy
   (1) 3-3/8" strip, into
     (5) 3-3/8" squares
   (4) 2" strips
   (3) 1-1/2" strips
Red
   (1) 3-3/8" strip, into
     (4) 3-3/8" squares
   (4) 1-1/2" strips
   (3) 1-1/4" strips

Background
   (2) 3-3/8" strips, into
     (16) 3-3/8" squares
     (6) 2-7/8" squares
   (1) 2-1/2" strip, into
     (12) 2-1/2" squares
   (1) 2" strip, into
     (12) 2" x 3-3/8"
Binding
   (3) 3" strips

Sewing

1. Make 12 SnS, Option 1, using 2-1/2" background squares and 1-1/2" red and navy corner strips. Sew red on two adjacent sides of each square and navy on the other two sides.

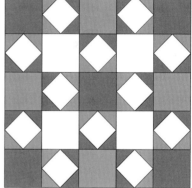

2. Arrange the 3-3/8" red, blue, and background squares with the SnS as shown below. Sew together in rows. Sew the rows together.

3. Make 6 SnS, Option 3, using 2-7/8" background squares and 1-1/2" corner strips of red and navy. Make 4 red SnS and 2 navy SnS.

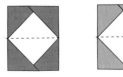

4. Sew the SnS halves from Step 3 to 2" x 3-3/8" background pieces, background side to background.

Using these units and 3-3/8" background squares, sew four rows of red unit, background, navy unit, background, and red unit. Add background squares to both ends of two of the rows.

Sew the short rows to opposite sides of the quilt. Sew the long rows to the top and bottom.

5. Sew on a border of 1-1/4" red following the border directions, page 8. Add a 2" navy border.

Montana Star

77" x 97"
Beginner
Photograph, page 22

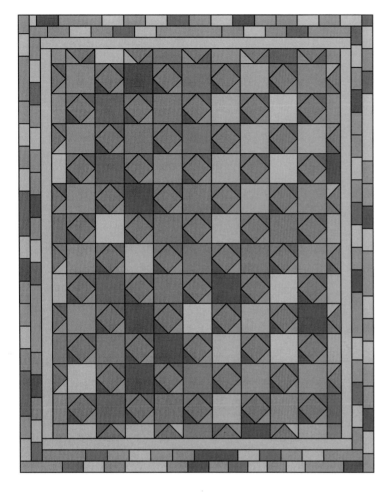

Autumn colors and country cotton prints give this quilt a spicy flare. Can you see the stars disappear before your very eyes? As soon as you find them, they're gone again! An easy Square in a Square™ pattern with a scrappy look makes this quilt practical and fun.

Yardage

9-1/3 yds.	Total scraps or fat quarters*
3/4 yd.	Inner border
7/8 yd.	Binding
5-7/8 yds.	Backing

*I used spicy, autumn, country prints in light, medium, and darks. Try for at least 12 to 18 different prints.

Cutting

Scraps
   (54) 6-7/8" squares
   (11) 5-3/8" squares
   (54) 5" squares
   (48) 2-3/4" strips
   (21) 3-3/4" x 6-7/8"
   (4) 3-3/4" squares
Inner Border
   (8) 2-3/4" strips
Binding
   (9) 3" strips

Sewing

1. Make 54 SnS, Option 1, using the 5" squares and 2-3/4" strips. Use different colors for the four corners.

2. Alternating the SnS from Step 1 and the 6-7/8" squares, sew six of each of the rows shown below.

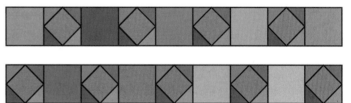

Sew the rows together.

3. Make 11 SnS, Option 3, using the 5-3/8" squares and 2-3/4" strips.

Sew these half SnS, the 3-3/4" x 6-7/8" rectangles, and 3-3/4" squares into rows for the edges of the quilt. Use the quilt diagram as a guide. Sew the long rows to the sides of the quilt. Add the short rows to the top and bottom.

4. Sew on the 2-3/4" inner border following the directions on page 8.

5. Cut scraps 2-3/4" wide by varying lengths. Piece these together to make two rows of pieced border for each edge of the quilt. You will need approximately 660" in length. Sew to the quilt as you would any border.

Pine Forest

34" x 41"
Beginner
Photograph, page 25

Yardage

(10) 4" squares	Trees, assorted
(6) 2" strips	Tree background, assorted
1/8 yd.	Tree trunks
1/2 yd.	Background
2/3 yd.	Sashing
1/8 yd.	Corners
1/2 yd.	Border
3/8 yd.	Binding
1-1/3 yds.	Backing

Cutting

Background
  (2) 4-1/2" strips, into spacers
    (2) 9" segments
    (1) 5-1/2" segments
    (12) 3-1/2" segments
  (1) 2-1/2" strip, into
    (4) 2-1/2" squares
  (2) 2" strips

Trees
  (10) 3-5/8" squares
Tree background
  (6) 2" strips
Tree trunks
  (1) 1-1/2" strip
Sashing
  (7) 3" strips
Corners
  (2) 1-1/2" strips
Border
  (4) 3-3/8" strips
Binding
  (4) 3" strips

Sewing

1. Make 10 SnS, Option 3, using the 3-5/8" tree squares and the 2" tree background strips.

2. Sew half SnS together to make tree stacks as follows: five with two per stack, two with three per stack, four are single halves.

3. Sew a 1-1/2" tree trunk strip between two 2" background strips. Crosscut this strip set into eleven 2-1/2" segments.

Add a trunk to each tree.

4. Sew trees and background spacers together in vertical rows following the diagram.

5. Find the average length of the rows (30-1/2"). Cut five 3" sashing strips this measurement. Stitch them between each row and on both sides.

6. Measure the width of the quilt through the center and cut two 3" sashing strips this length. Sew them to the top and bottom of the quilt.

7. Make 4 SnS, Option 1, using the 2-1/2" background squares and 1-1/2" corner strips.

8. Cut two 3-3/8" border strips the length of the quilt and two the width. Sew on the side borders. Sew an SnS from Step 7 to each end of the top and bottom borders. Stitch these to the quilt.

11

All Spruced Up

12" x 14"
Beginner
Photograph, page 25

Have you ever tried to sew triangles that are 1" on the angle? Most of us would never even try it! But with the Square in a Square™ way, this little tree is picture perfect. It can be "All Spruced Up" before Christmas Eve.

Yardage

1/4 yd. Green
1/8 yd. Light print
1/3 yd. Red
      Small scraps for presents
1/4 yd. Background
1/4 yd. Binding
1/2 yd. Backing

Cutting

With the small pieces in this quilt, it is easier to cut as you sew, therefore cutting instructions are with the sewing directions.

Sewing

1. Cut (10) 1-1/4" light print squares
   Cut (2) 1" green strips

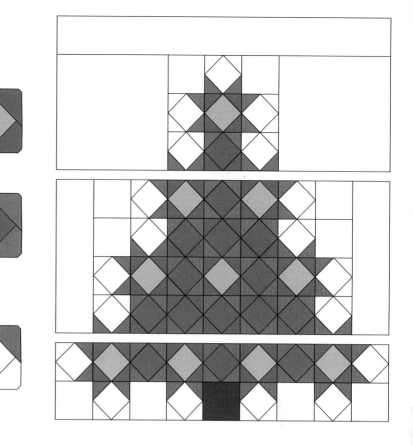

Make 10 SnS, Option 1. Press and set aside.

2. Cut (6) 1-1/4" green squares
   Cut (2) 1" red strips

Make 6 SnS, Option 1.

3. Cut (2) 1" red strips
   From background -
      Cut (19) 1-1/4" squares
      Cut (2) 1" strips

Make 19 SnS, Option 1, with two adjacent red corners and two background corners.

4. Cut (1) 1" red strip
   From green -
      Cut (9) 1-1/4" green squares
      Cut (1) 1" green strip

Make 9 SnS, Option 1, with two adjacent red corners and two green corners.

5. Cut (1) 1-1/2" green square
   From background -
      Cut (2) 3-1/2" squares
      Cut (1) 1-1/2" x 9-1/2" rectangle
      Cut (2) 1-1/2" x 4-1/2" rectangles
      Cut (10) 1-1/2" squares

Sew tree together in sections as shown at the right.

6. Cut (4) assorted 1" x 5" strips for bows
   Cut (1) 1-1/2" green square
   Cut (2) 1" x 1-1/4" presents
   Cut (1) 2-1/2" x 1-1/4" present
   Cut (1) 1-1/2" x 1" present
   From background -
      Cut (2) 3/4" squares
      Cut (2) 1-1/4" squares
      Cut (3) 1-1/2" squares
      Cut (2) 1-1/4" x 3/4" rectangles
      Cut (1) 1-1/2" x 3/4" rectangles
      Cut (2) 1" x 1-1/2" rectangles

Make 2 SnS, Option 3, for bow tops. Use the two 1-1/4" background squares and the 1" x 5" strips. Have two adjacent corner strips on each square the same fabric.

Assemble the bottom row following the diagram below. Sew it to the bottom of the tree.

7. Cut (3) 1-1/4" red border strips
   Cut (8) 1-1/4" green squares

Cut two border strips the length of the quilt and two the width of the quilt. Sew on the side borders. Stitch a green square to both ends of the top and bottom borders. Sew them on the quilt. Repeat these steps, adding another border of the same fabric with green squares in the corners.

Water Wheel

71" x 94"
Beginner
Photograph, page 26

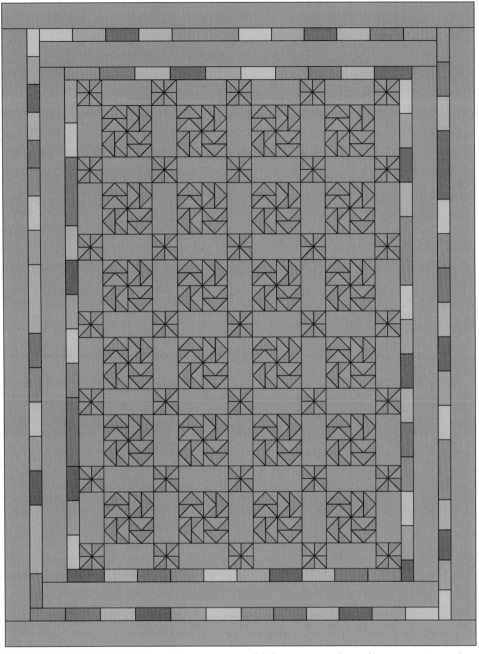

Cutting

Wheels
- (1) 3-3/4" strip per fabric, into
  - (48) 3-3/4" squares (4 per fabric)
  - (35) 3-5/8" squares, assorted remainder into 2" strips
- (2) 2" strips per fabric

Background
- (6) 8-1/2" strips, into
  - (58) 8-1/2" x 4"
- (8) 4-1/2" strips
- (7) 4" strips
- (5) 3-3/4" strips, into
  - (48) 3-3/4" squares
- (26) 2" strips
- (18) 1-7/8" strips

Color Border
- (15) 2" strips

Binding
- (8) 3" strips

This quilt is known by many names. Using my color placement and the coolness of the look, I felt an antique Water Wheel was it's calling. You will enjoy making this in a variety of colors. Watch out, it goes together fast.

Yardage

1/4 yd.	Each of 12 wheel prints
6-3/4 yds.	Background
1 yd.	Color border, assorted
3/4 yd.	Binding
5-5/8 yds.	Backing

Sewing

There are 24 water wheel blocks. Make two of each wheel color.

1. Make 48 SnS, Option 3, using the 3-3/4" wheel squares and the 2" background strips. Repeat with the 3-3/4" background squares and the 2" wheel strips.

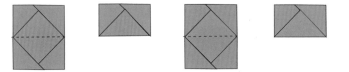

2. Sew the wheel and background half SnS together in same color pairs to make units. Make eight units of each wheel color. Sew with the large wheel triangle on the bottom and the large background triangle on top. This allows you to see the tip of the triangle so you will not sew it off.

Sew four same color units together to make a water wheel block. Make 24 blocks.

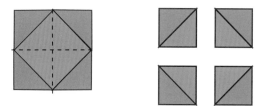

3. Make 35 SnS, Option 4, using the 3-5/8" wheel squares and the 1-7/8" background strips.

Sew the half square triangles together to make 35 pinwheel blocks.

4. Lay the water wheel blocks, the pinwheels, and the 8-1/2" x 4" background sashing pieces out in a pleasing arrangement. Join the water wheel blocks and sashing in vertical rows, as shown to the right.

Likewise, sew the pinwheel blocks and sashing in vertical rows.

Now sew the rows together.

5. Cut the 2" border strips into varying lengths. Piece these together to make a scrap border. You will need about 555" in length. Sew on the four borders following the directions on page 8.

Border 1 - 2" scrap

Border 2 - 4" background

Border 3 - 2" scrap

Border 4 - 4-1/2" background

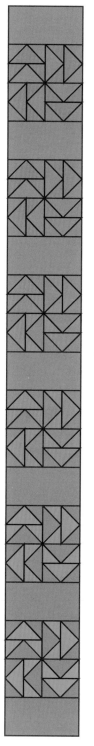

Chain of Hearts

21" x 21"
Beginner
Photograph, page 23

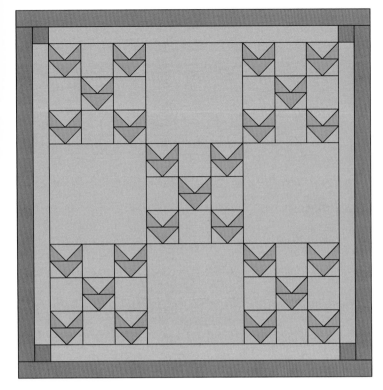

Our lives should be a chain of love, just like this quilt. One heart right after the other giving love and receiving. I'm so very thankful that I have a never ending chain of hearts in my life.

Yardage

1/4 yd.	Each of 4 heart fabrics
5/8 yd.	Background
1/4 yd.	Border
1/3 yd.	Binding
3/4 yd.	Backing

Cutting

Hearts
   (13) 2" squares, assorted
   (1) 1-1/4" strip of each fabric
Background
   (1) 5-3/8" strip, into
      (4) 5-3/8" squares
      (13) 2" squares
   (1) 2-1/8" strip, into
      (20) 2-1/8" squares
   (2) 2" strips
   (4) 1-1/4" strips

16

Border
   (3) 2" strips
Binding
   (3) 3" strips

Sewing

1. Make 26 SnS following the directions for Option 3. Make 13 using 2" background squares and 1-1/4" red corner strips. Alternate the different red fabrics on the square. Now make 13 using 2" red squares and 1-1/4" background corner strips.

2. Sew 25 hearts using two half SnS for each, one with a background center square and one with a red center.

3. Make five 9-patch blocks alternating 2-1/8" background squares with heart squares.

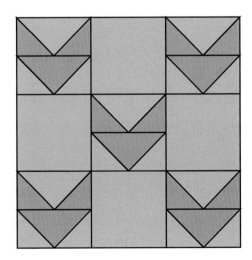

4. Sew the heart blocks and the 5-3/8" background squares together into a bigger 9-patch.

5. Measure and cut top, bottom, and side borders from 2" background. Sew side borders on. Cut four 2" squares from the border fabric. Sew to the ends of the top and bottom borders and stitch to the quilt. Add 2" border to all four sides.

Disappearing Star

54" x 72"
Beginner
Photograph, back cover

Yardage

1/4 yd.	Each of 12 (green, blue, red)
1/3 yd.	Each of 10 background
1/3 yd.	Each of 5 (dark brown, large squares)
1 yd.	Border
2/3 yd.	Binding
3-1/3 yds.	Backing

Cutting

Green, blue, red
(7) 5" squares, assorted
(13) 2-3/4" strips, assorted
(6) 2-3/4" x 13", assorted
Background
(2) 3-5/8" strips of each fabric
(6) 2-3/4" x 13" strips, assorted

Dark brown
(17) 9-1/2" squares, assorted
Border
(6) 5" strips
Binding
(7) 3" strips

Sewing

1. Make 7 SnS, Option 1, using the 5" squares and the 2-3/4" green, blue, and red strips. Make the four corners of each block the same fabric. Sew 3-5/8" background strips around the SnS block, Option 2, varying the fabrics in the corners.

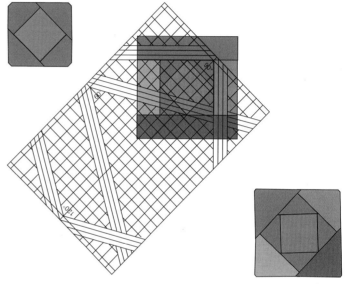

2. Sew six 2-3/4" x 13" colored strips to six 2-3/4" x 13" background strips, making six pairs. Cross cut four 2-3/4" segments from each pair. Sew these segments into eleven 4-patch squares.

Sew 2-3/4" colored strips to the 4-patches to make SnS, Option 1. Add 3-5/8" background strips and trim, Option 2.

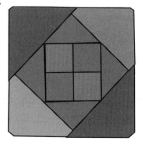

3. Arrange the SnS blocks and the 9-1/2" dark brown blocks into seven rows of five, alternating blocks and colors. Stitch together.

4. Attach the 5" border according to the border directions, page 8.

Nine Patch

60" x 77"
Beginner

A 9-patch can be used in many ways. It is practical and easy for beginners, yet versatile enough to keep experienced quilters challenged. In this quilt the 9-patch substitutes for the center square in the Square in a Square™ block.

Yardage

2-1/2 yds.	Total scraps, assorted medium to dark fabrics*
4 yds.	Total background, assorted
1/2 yd.	Inner border
1-1/3 yds.	Outer border
2/3 yd.	Binding
3-2/3 yds.	Backing

*Over 24 different fabrics were used in black, brown, tan, red, blue, and gold.

Cutting

Scraps
  Included in sewing instructions
Background
  (35) 3-1/2" strips, assorted
Inner border
  (6) 2-1/2" strips
Outer border
  (7) 6" strips
Binding
  (7) 3" strips

Sewing

1. Make 35 different 9-patch blocks. You can cut 2-1/2" squares to piece the blocks or use short strip sets. The strip set method is explained here. For each two blocks cut three 2-1/2" x 8" strips of two different fabrics. Sew two strip sets along the long edges as shown. Cut three 2-1/2" segments from each strip set and sew into two opposite 9-patch blocks.

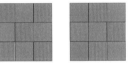

2. Sew 3-1/2" background strips to the 9-patch blocks to make SnS, Option 1. Use four different background fabrics for each block.

3. Sew the blocks into seven rows of five blocks.

4. Sew on the 2-1/2" inner border according to the border directions, page 8.

5. The second border is a 1-1/2" scrap border. You may simply sew 1-1/2" scraps of varying lengths together to make this border. Use both the background and other scraps. I added half square triangles periodically in the border. You can make the half square triangles using the SnS method. For 40 half square triangles cut ten 2-5/8" center squares. Sew assorted 1-3/8" corner strips on and cut as directed for Option 4.

6. Sew on the 6" outer border.

Prairie Claw

89" x 100"
Intermediate
Photograph on cover

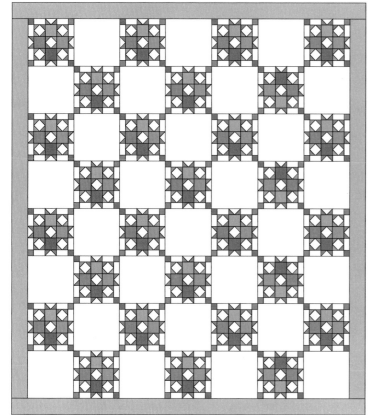

This reproduction of the traditional Devil's Claw pattern is appealing with its many star points and dark fabrics. Visualize a covered wagon rolling across the prairie, with an occasional weed named devil's claw clinging to a turning wheel or skirt tail.

Yardage

3-1/3 yds.	Red (1/3 yd. each of 10)
1-1/3 yds.	Black (1/3 yd. each of 4)
1/3 yd.	Gold
5-5/8 yds.	Background
1-1/8 yds.	Border
1 yd.	Binding
8 yds.	Backing

Cutting

Red, black & gold
    (112) 3-3/8" squares, assorted
    (112) 2" squares, assorted
    (73) 1-1/2" strips, assorted

Background
    (10) 12-1/8" strips, into
        (28) 12-1/8" squares
        (76) 2-1/2" squares
    (11) 3-3/8" strips, into
        (224) 3-3/8" x 2"
    (4) 2-7/8" strips, into
        (56) 2-7/8" squares
    (4) 2-1/2" strips, into
        (64) 2-1/2" squares
Border
    (9) 4" strips
Binding
    (10) 3" strips

Sewing

1. Make 140 (5 per block) SnS, Option 1. Use the 2-1/2" background squares and the 1-1/2" colored strips. Sew a different color strip to each side of the square.

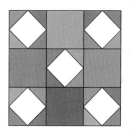

2. Make (28) 9-patch blocks, using five SnS and four 3-3/8" colored squares each.

3. Make 56 (2 per block) SnS, Option 3. Use the 2-7/8" background squares and 1-1/2" colored strips. Sew different colored strips to each side of the square.

4. Sew each of the half SnS between two 3-3/8" x 2" background rectangles. Sew half of these units to opposite sides of the blocks.

Stitch a 2" colored square to each end of the remaining units. Sew these to the top and bottom of the blocks.

5. Sew eight rows of seven blocks, alternating pieced blocks and 12-1/8" background squares. Sew the rows together.

6. Add the 4" border according to the directions on page 8.

19

Kansas Windmill

77" x 95"
Beginner
Photograph, page 21

I was born on the prairie, therefore the windmill is a welcome and familiar sight. You can see them everywhere across the rolling hills. Being a Kansan, born on Kansas' birthday, the windmill just had to go in the book, and with sunflower fabric, no less!

Yardage

6 yds.	Total windmills, assorted
4-1/8 yds.	Background
1/2 yd.	Border
7/8 yd.	Binding
5-2/3 yds.	Backing

Cutting

Background
   (16) 4-1/8" strips, into
      (15) 4-1/8" x 15"
      (48) 4-1/8" x 7-3/4"
   (8) 4-1/8" sashing strips
   (8) 4-1/2" border strips

Windmills
   (45) 6" squares, assorted
   (45) 3-1/4" strips, assorted
Border
   (7) 2-1/4" strips
Binding
   (9) 3" strips

Sewing

1. The windmills are made with different color combinations. Each windmill block requires 2 SnS blocks with the same color center square and the corner strips of one color. Follow the SnS instructions, Option 3. Use 24 of the 6" squares and about 24 of the 3-1/4" strips to make twelve blocks.

Sew each half SnS to a 4-1/8" x 7-3/4" background. Lay the half SnS on top, when sewing, so you can see the tip and avoid sewing it off.

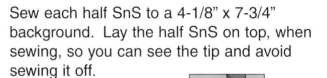

Sew four of these units together to make each block. Make twelve.

2. Sew the blocks together in vertical rows with 4-1/8" x 15" background sashing between and on the ends.

Sew the rows together with 4-1/8" background strips between and on both sides.

3. Attach the 2-1/4" border following the border instructions, page 8.

4. Make 21 SnS, Option 3, using the remaining 6" squares and 3-1/4" strips. Vary the colors of the corner strips on each square. Sew together eleven half SnS to make a long border. Sew it to one long side of the quilt. Next sew together two long borders of nine half SnS each. Stitch these to the top and bottom. Now sew twelve half SnS together for the remaining long side.

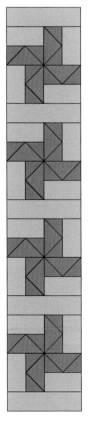

5. Sew the last border, 4-1/2" background strips, to the quilt.

Kansas Windmill

77" x 95"

Montana Star

77" x 97"

Sea of Galilee
14" x 16"

Berry Baskets
45" x 45"

Chain of Hearts
21" x 21"

Constellation
25" x 25"

Desert Star
74" x 86"

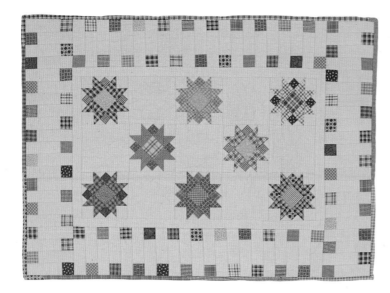

Mini Sawtooth Star
20" x 27"

Pine Forest
34" x 41"

All Spruced Up
12" x 14"

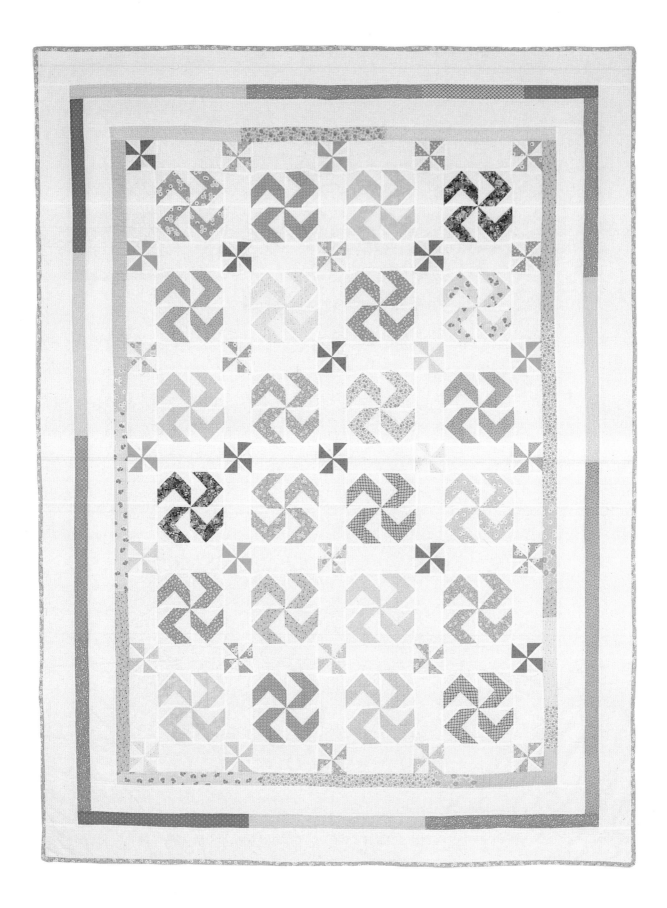

Water Wheel

71" x 94"

Revolving Star

85" x 102"

Prairie Star

77" x 77"

Prairie Star
77" x 77"
Advanced
Photograph, page 28

Most of our quilts will out live us. This quilt could be passed down to many generations. Your love will warm their hearts and souls long after you are gone.

Yardage

2/3 yd.	Each of 8 stars
3-5/8 yds.	Background
1 yd.	Border
3/4 yd.	Binding
4-2/3 yds.	Backing

Cutting

Stars
 (52) 3-3/4" squares, multiples of 4
 (57) 1-3/4" strips, assorted
 (17) 1-7/8" strips, assorted
Background
 (6) 14-1/2" strips, into
  (12) 14-1/2" squares
  (13) 4" squares
  (52) 3" squares
  (52) 2-1/4" squares
 (3) 4" strips, into
  (52) 4" x 2-1/4"
 (5) 3-3/8" strips, into
  (52) 3-3/8" squares

Border
 (8) 4" strips
Binding
 (8) 3" strips

Sewing

Make 13 different prairie star blocks. Each block uses two star fabrics. Decide on the combinations.

1. Make 52 (4 each combination) SnS, Option 1. Use the 3" background squares and the 1-3/4" star strips. Alternate the two colors on the background square as shown.

2. Make 52 SnS, Option 3, using the 3-3/8" background squares and the 1-3/4" star strips. Make four of each color combination used in Step 1. Cut all four squares with the same color placement.

3. Make 52 SnS, Option 4, using the 3-3/4" star squares and 1-7/8" star strips. Make four of each color combination used in Steps 1 and 2. Sew four of these half square triangles together to make the centers of the stars. Make sure the pieces are turned so that when the half SnS are sewn on, like colors are touching.

4. Assemble the blocks using the units from Steps 1, 2, and 3. Also use background pieces as follows: one 4" square, four 2-1/4" squares and four 2-1/4" x 4" pieces per block.

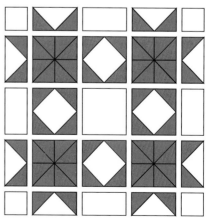

5. Sew five rows of five blocks, alternating pieced blocks and 14-1/2" background squares. Sew the rows together.

6. Add the 4" border according to the directions on page 8.

Winter Turkey Tracks

94" x 94"
Intermediate

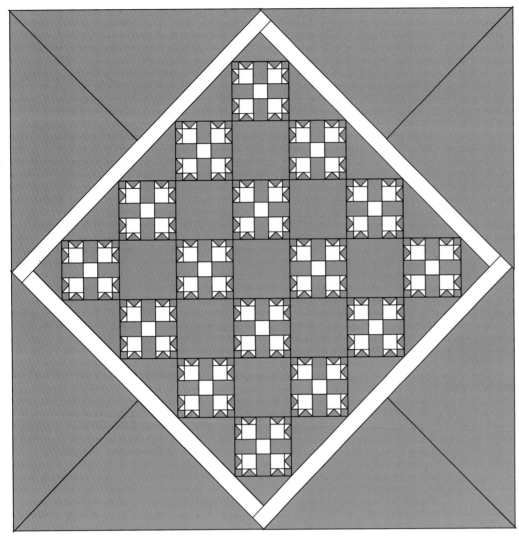

Turkey Tracks is a traditional pattern often done in red and white. A blue and white one reminds me of tracks in winter snow. This quilt can be sewn before your turkey dinner is thawed and basted.

Cutting

Main
- (7) 3-1/8" strips, into
  - (80) 3-1/8" squares
- (7) 3-1/8" strips, border
- (26) 1-1/2" strips

Background
- (2) 11-1/8" strips, into
  - (6) 11-1/8" squares
- Trim selvage from one edge of remaining length.
- Cut full length of fabric 24" wide (24" x 220"). Set aside.
- From remaining (approx. 18" width) cut
  - (3) 16-1/2" squares
  - (3) 11-1/8" squares
  - (2) 8-1/2" squares
  - (13) 4-1/2" strips (18"), into
    - (64) 3-1/8" x 4-1/2"
  - (11) 2-3/4" x 18" strips, into
    - (64) 2-3/4" squares
  - (8) 1-7/8" x 18" strips, into
    - (64) 1-7/8" squares

Binding
- (10) 3" strips

Yardage

7-1/2 yds.	Background
2-5/8 yds.	Main
1 yd.	Binding
8-1/2 yds.	Backing

Sewing

1. Make 64 SnS, Option 3. Use the 2-3/4" background squares and 1-1/2" main strips.

2. Stitch 64 of the half SnS to 1-7/8" background squares, as shown.

Sew the other 64 half SnS to 3-1/8" main squares. Stitch along the point side of the large triangle as shown.

Sew the half SnS units together.

3. Sew two of the units from Step 2 to each of 32 of the 3-1/8" x 4-1/2" background pieces.

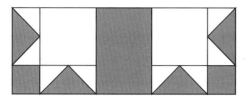

Stitch each remaining 3-1/8" main square between two 3-1/8" x 4-1/2" background pieces.

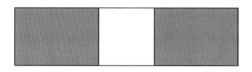

Sew these units into 16 blocks.

4. Cut the 16-1/2" background squares into fourths, diagonally.

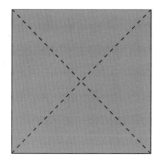

Cut the 8-1/2 background squares in half diagonally.

Lay the quilt out in diagonal rows as shown in the diagram, alternating pieced blocks and 11-1/8" background blocks. Lay a large background triangle from before at both ends of each row, with the straight grain edge to the outside of the quilt. Lay the smaller background triangles in the corners. Sew the blocks and triangles into rows. Stitch the rows together.

Trim and square up the quilt. Trim the edges 1/4" from the points of the pieced blocks.

5. Sew on the 3-1/8" main border according to the directions on page 8.

6. From the long background strip (24" x 220") cut eight corner triangles. Along one long edge make a mark every 48". On the opposite edge make a mark 24" from the short edge, then every 48". Cut as shown at right.

Sew the triangles together in pairs.

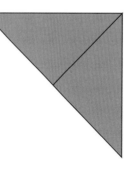

Sew these large triangles to the sides of the quilt centering the seam of the triangle on each side.

Goose Paw

77" x 105"
Intermediate

The Bear Paw looks good with any fabric choice. Sharp claw points and no bias stretch are quick and sure with the Square in a Square™ way of sewing and cutting. This technique turns the Bear Paw into the Goose Paw.

Yardage

3-1/2 yds.	Each of two paw fabrics, A & B
3-2/3 yds.	Background
2 yds.	Centers & outer border
7/8 yd.	Binding
6-1/4 yds.	Backing

Cutting

Paws - Cut from each fabric, A & B
    (6) 4-1/2" strips, into
        (48) 4-1/2" squares
    (1) 2-1/2" strip, into
        (12) 2-1/2" squares
    (23) 2-1/8" strips
    (17) 2" strips
Background
    (6) 4" strips, into
        (60) 4" squares
    (7) 3-5/8" strips, into
        (76) 3-5/8" squares
    (7) 3-1/2" border strips
    (18) 2-1/2" strips, into
        (38) 2-1/2" x 12-1/2"
        (20) 2-1/2" x 6-1/2"
        (16) 2-1/2" x 4-1/2"
        (4) 2-1/2" squares
Center & outer border
    (2) 4-1/2" strips, into
        (15) 4-1/2" squares
    (9) 6" border strips
Binding
    (9) 3" strips

Sewing

1. Make 76 SnS, Option 3, using the 3-5/8" background squares and 2-1/8" paw strips. Sew the A paw fabric to two adjacent sides of the square and the B fabric to the other two sides. Carefully cut for Option 3 as shown. Be sure to leave 1/4" seam allowance on corners where A and B meet. Cut to the point on corners that are both A or both B. You'll have 76 half SnS with A on the left and 76 with B on the left.

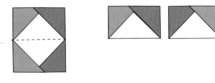

2. Sew these half SnS in pairs to make 38 A units and 38 B units.

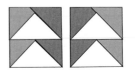

3. Make 15 blocks. Use two A units, two B units, two 4-1/2" A paw squares, two 4-1/2" B paw squares, and a 4-1/2" center square. Arrange all the blocks in the same order. Make sure claw points are the same fabric as the paw.

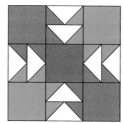

4. Make 60 SnS, Option 4, using 4" background squares and 2" paw strips. This will yield 240 half square triangles. Make 30 with A strips and 30 with B strips. Press gently, don't stretch.

5. Make four corner blocks, two each of paw fabrics A and B. Use four half square triangles, one 4-1/2" paw square, and one 2-1/2" background square for each.

6. Make 16 half blocks. Use a 4-1/2" paw square of each color, two half square triangles of each color, a unit from Step 2, and a 2-1/2" x 4-1/2" background for each. Make eight with fabric A on the left and eight with fabric A on the right.

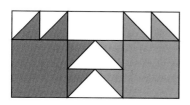

7. Lay out all the blocks, half blocks and corner units, matching the A and B fabrics. Stitch together in vertical rows with 2-1/2" x 12-1/2" background between blocks, and 2-1/2" x 6-1/2" background between half blocks.

8. Sew together four long sashing rows using five 2-1/2" x 12-1/2" background, two 2-1/2" x 6-1/2" background, three 2-1/2" A paw squares, and three 2-1/2" B paw squares for each. Alternate the A and B paw squares. Sew these between the vertical rows, reversing every other row so the squares match the color of the surrounding paw.

9. Sew on the 3-1/2" background border following the directions on page 8.

10. The remaining half square triangles are for the next border. You may have them go around the quilt randomly, run off the quilt, or go around clockwise. Play with the placement of the corners squares. Have fun! Sew them together in long strips and stitch to the quilt.

11. Add the 6" outer border.

Berry Baskets

45" x 45"
Intermediate
Photograph, page 23

Cutting

Baskets - Cut for each two
  baskets
    (2) 3" squares
    (1) 1-3/8" x 35" strip
    (1) 1-1/2" x 35" strip
Background
    (1) 8-1/2" strip, into
        (3) 8-1/2" squares
        (2) 4-1/2" squares
    (2) 3" strips, into
        (17) 3" squares
    (3) 2-5/8" strips, into
        (33) 2-5/8" squares
    (8) 1-3/4" strips, into
        (66) 1-3/4" x 3"
        (66) 1-3/4" squares
First border
    (4) 2" strips
Second border
    (3) 7-1/2" strips, into
        (8) 12-1/2" x 7-1/2"
    (7) 3" strips
Binding
    (5) 3" strips

Quilts and baskets—two of my very favorite things. Most of us think little quilts are so cute, so you can imagine how excited I was with this little basket quilt. Triangles won't be a bother with the Square in a Square™ way of piecing a quilt.

Yardage

1/8 yd.	Each of 17 basket fabrics*
1-1/8 yds.	Background
1/4 yd.	First border
1-1/3 yds.	Second border
1/2 yd.	Binding
2-7/8 yds.	Backing

*Scraps and fat quarters work too. You get two baskets from 1/8 yd. fabric.

Sewing

1. Make 33 SnS, Option 3, using 2-5/8" background squares and 1-3/8" basket strips. Make all four corners the same color. One SnS makes basket points for one basket.

2. Sew one basket point to a same color 3" square. Sew the other basket point to a 1-3/4" background square.

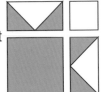

Sew these units together.

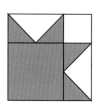

3. Make 17 SnS, Option 4, for basket feet. Use 3" squares of background and 1-1/2" basket strips. Make all four corners the same color. Each SnS makes feet for two baskets.

Sew a 1-3/4" x 3" background to each foot. Sew a mirror-image pair for each basket. Now sew a 1-3/4" background square to the other side of one basket foot.

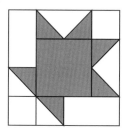

Sew the short foot strip to one side of the basket. Stitch the long foot strip to the other side.

4. Cut the 8-1/2" background squares in quarters, diagonally.

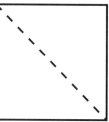

Cut the 4-1/2" background squares in half, diagonally.

Lay out 25 of the blocks in a pleasing arrangement as shown in the diagram. They will be on point. Place the background triangles cut from the 8-1/2" square along the edges, straight grain to the outside edge. Place the smaller triangles in the corners.

Sew the blocks together in diagonal rows. Sew the rows together. Trim and square up the outside edges.

5. Sew on the 2" first border following the directions on page 8.

6. Use the remaining eight basket blocks to make SnS, Option 1. Use 3" second border strips. These are for the border.

Sew a 12-1/2" x 7-1/2" second border piece to the top and bottom of two basket blocks. Stitch these to the sides of the quilt. Sew a 12-1/2" x 7-1/2" second border piece to both sides of two basket blocks. Add a basket block to the ends of each unit. Sew these to the top and bottom of the quilt.

Snails Tails
72" x 84"
Intermediate

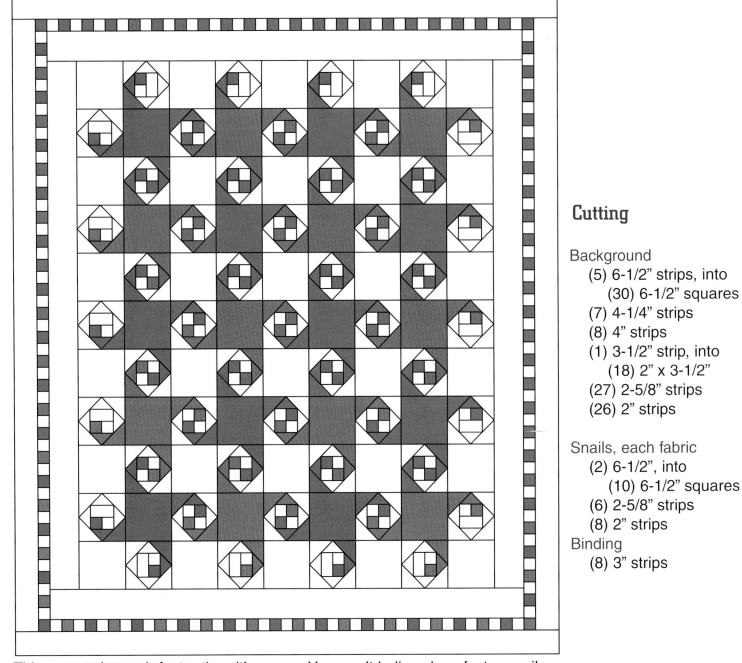

Cutting

Background
- (5) 6-1/2" strips, into
  - (30) 6-1/2" squares
- (7) 4-1/4" strips
- (8) 4" strips
- (1) 3-1/2" strip, into
  - (18) 2" x 3-1/2"
- (27) 2-5/8" strips
- (26) 2" strips

Snails, each fabric
- (2) 6-1/2", into
  - (10) 6-1/2" squares
- (6) 2-5/8" strips
- (8) 2" strips

Binding
- (8) 3" strips

This pattern is much faster than it's name. You won't believe how fast a snail can be, using the Square in a Square™ technique.

Yardage

1-3/8 yds.	Snail A
1-3/8 yds.	Snail B
6-3/4 yds.	Background
3/4 yd.	Binding
5-1/8 yds.	Backing

Sewing

1. Sew two 2" snail A and two 2" snail B strips each to a 2" background strip. Crosscut into (40) 2" sections of each color.

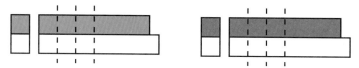

2. Make (31) 4-patch units using a snail A and a snail B unit from Step 1 for each.

3. Make 31 SnS, Option 1, using the units from Step 2 as the center square. Sew 2" snail strips on opposite sides first, matching snail colors. Then stitch background strips on the other two sides.

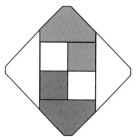

4. Add another row of strips, Option 2, to the units in Step 3. Use the 2-5/8" strips and begin with the snail strips first as shown. Add the background strips.

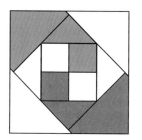

5. Sew the remaining units from Step 1 to a 2" x 3-1/2" background.

6. Make 18 SnS, Option 1, using the units from Step 5 and 2" snail and background strips. First sew a snail strip to the same color snail square in the center. Add background strips to the other three sides.

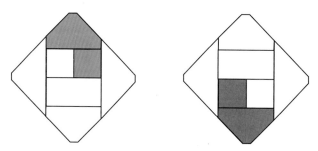

7. Add a row of 2-5/8" strips, Option 2, to the units from Step 6. Sew on a snail strip first, as shown, then add background strips to the other three sides.

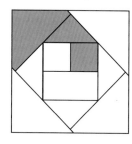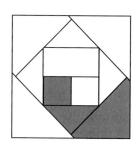

8. Carefully lay out the units from Steps 4 and 7 with 6-1/2" squares of snail A, snail B, and background as shown in the diagram. Alternate snail colors and make sure the color flows correctly.

Stitch the eleven rows of nine blocks. Sew the rows together.

9. Add the 4-1/4" background border according to the directions on page 8.

10. Use the remaining 2" strips to sew two strip sets as shown below. Crosscut them into 2" segments. Also crosscut the remaining strip set from Step 1.

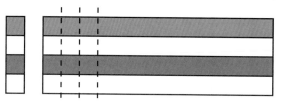

11. Sew the segments together to make long border strips which alternate the snail colors around the quilt.

Sew on the side borders, then the top and bottom.

12. Add the 4" background border.

37

Revolving Star

85" x 102"
Advanced
Photograph, page 27

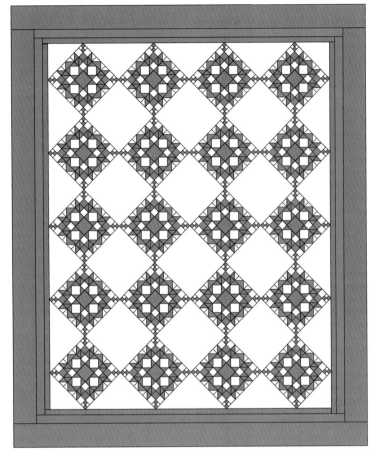

This block is easier than it looks. With the Square in a Square™ technique the parts are made and sewn together with ease.

Yardage

4-1/8 yds.	Main (black)
3-1/8 yds.	Accent (blue)
6-1/4 yds.	Background
1 yd.	Binding
7-2/3 yds.	Backing

Cutting

Main
(9) 6" strips
(7) 3-3/8" strips, into
    (80) 3-3/8" squares
(2) 3-1/2" strips, into
    (20) 3-1/2" squares
(8) 1-3/4" strips
(16) 1-5/8" strips
(5) 1-1/4" strips

Accent
(3) 3" strips, into
    (40) 3" squares
(8) 2-1/2" strips
(4) 2" strips
(21) 1-3/4" strips
(16) 1-5/8" strips
Background
(2) 18-1/2" strips, into
    (4) 18-1/2" squares
(4) 12-1/2" strips, into
    (12) 12-1/2" squares
(1) 9-1/2" strip, into
    (2) 9-1/2" squares
    (24) 2-5/8" squares
(4) 2-5/8" strips, into
    (56) 2-5/8" squares
(8) 2" strips, into
    (160) 2" squares
(4) 2" strips
(21) 1-3/4" strips
(18) 1-5/8" strips
(5) 1-1/4" strips
Binding
(10) 3" strips

Sewing

1. Sew each 1-1/4" main strip to a 1-1/4" background strip. Press and crosscut (160) 1-1/4" slices. Sew the slices together in pairs to make (80) 4-patch units.

2. Sew the units from Step 1 to 2" background squares. Make sure the 4-patch is turned as shown.

Sew each of the 2" accent strips to a 2" background strip. Press and crosscut (80) 2" slices.

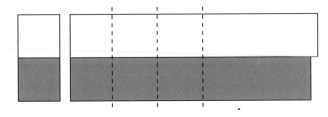

Sew the units together to make 80 large 4-patch units.

3. Make 80 SnS, Option 4, using the 3-3/8" main squares and the 1-3/4" strips of accent and background. Make 40 with accent strips and 40 with background strips.

Sew each main/background half square triangle to a main/accent one. Make 80 as shown at left and 80 as at right.

 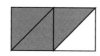

Stitch the left units to 2" background squares, with the accent fabric next to the square.

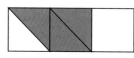

4. Assemble the corner blocks using all the units made so far. Make 80.

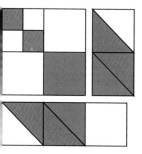 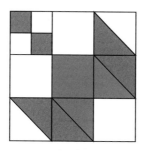

5. Make 80 SnS, Option 1, using 2-5/8" background squares and 1-5/8" strips of main and accent. Sew a main strip to the first side and an accent strip to the opposite side. The third side is a main strip and the fourth an accent.

6. Make 40 SnS, Option 3, using 3" accent squares and 1-5/8" background strips.

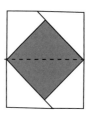

7. Assemble the blocks using the corner blocks from Step 4, the SnS from Step 5, the half SnS from Step 6, and the 3-1/2" main squares.

8. Cut the 18-1/2" background squares into quarters, diagonally.

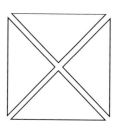

Cut the 9-1/2" background squares in half, diagonally.

Lay the blocks out, on point, in five rows of four. Place 12-1/2" background squares between the blocks. Put the larger background triangles along the edges and the smaller triangles in the corners, as shown.

Stitch the quilt in diagonal rows. Sew the rows together.

9. Sew the borders on according to the directions on page 8.
1st border - 1-3/4" main
2nd border - 2-1/2" accent
3rd border - 6" main

Sawtooth Star

105" x 105"
Advanced

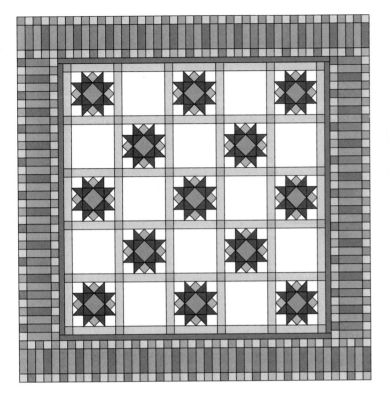

One of my favorite quilts is the Sister's Choice block with a piano border. It is a fun and exciting quilt to put together; a real showpiece for your collection. This is a scrap quilt, with each of the stars different.

Yardage

1/4 yd.	Each of 11-15 medium (star)
1/2 yd.	Each of 7 dark (star)
1 yd.	Each of 9 background
5/8 yd.	Border
1 yd.	Binding
9-3/8 yds.	Backing

Cutting

Medium
  Stars
    (13) 5" squares, assorted
    (52) 2-3/4" squares (4 of same color per block)
  Sashing and border
    (36) 2-7/8" squares, assorted
  Piano border
    (156) 2-7/8" squares, assorted
Dark
  (35) 2-3/4" strips (5 each, for 2 blocks)
Background
  Stars
    (52) 3-5/8" squares (4 same color per block)
    (104) 2-3/4" squares (8 same color per block)
  Plain blocks, sashing, and border
    (12) 13" squares
    (60) 13" x 2-7/8"
  Piano border
    (156) 2-7/8" squares - assorted backgrounds
    (156) 7-5/8" x 2-7/8" - assorted backgrounds
Border (step 5) (8) 2-1/2"
Binding
  (11) 3" strips

Sewing

Make 13 different stars. Each star uses two mediums, a dark, and a background. You may wish to mix the background within a block.

1. Make 13 SnS, Options 1, using 5" medium center squares and 2-3/4" dark strips for each. Use the same color strips for all four corners .

2. Sew two 2-3/4" background squares to each 2-3/4" medium square as shown here.

Stitch 2-3/4" same color dark strips to two sides of this unit as shown, Option 6. Trim, leaving 1/4" seam allowance on all sides.

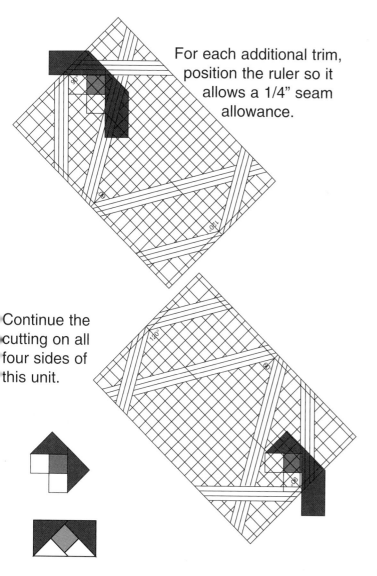

For each additional trim, position the ruler so it allows a 1/4" seam allowance.

Continue the cutting on all four sides of this unit.

Sew the rows together with a sashing strip between.

Sew two sashing strips using five 13" x 2-7/8" background and six 2-7/8" medium squares each, for the sides. Sew to the sides of the quilt.

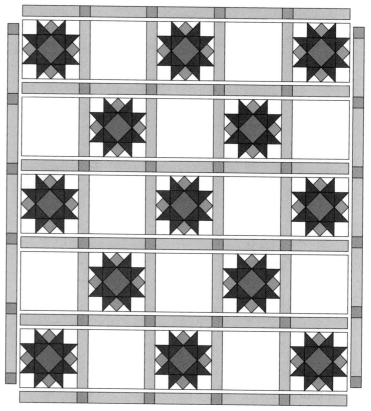

3. Sew the stars together using the units from Steps 1 and 2 and the 3-5/8" background squares.

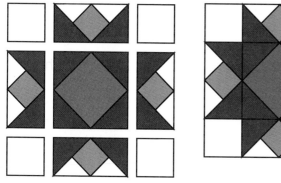

4. Sew the blocks, the 13" background squares, and 13" x 2-7/8" background into five rows of five, alternating blocks and squares as shown in the diagram.

Sew six horizontal sashing strips using five 13" x 2-7/8" background and four 2-7/8" medium squares each, as shown in the diagram.

5. Following the border directions, page 8, sew on a 2-1/2" border.

6. Sew a 2-7/8" medium square to one end of each 7-5/8" x 2-7/8" background. Stitch a 2-7/8" background square to the other end. These pieces are indicated by light grays in the illustrations.

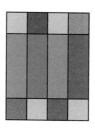

Sew two sets of 34 of these units together along the long sides to make side borders. Alternate the placement of the medium square. Stitch them to the sides of the quilt. Sew two sets of 44 units for the top and bottom. Stitch them to the quilt.

Mini Sawtooth Star

20" x 27"
Advanced
Photograph, page 25

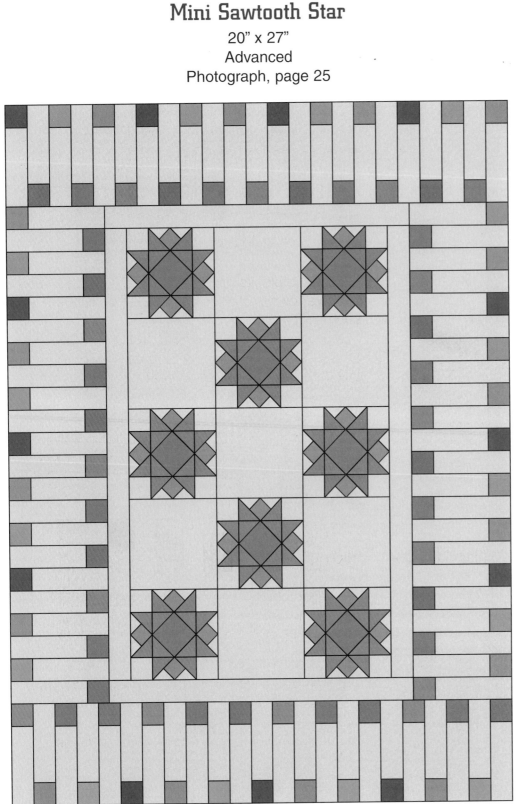

Cutting

Each star uses three fabrics.
For each one of the eight
stars cut:
Center square
    (1) 1-3/4" square
    (4) 1-3/8" squares
Star points
    (1) 1-1/8" strip
    (4) 1-3/8" squares
Outer square
    (4) 1-1/8" squares
    (4) 1-3/8" squares
Background
    (1) 4" strip, into
      (7) 4" squares
    (9) 1-3/8" strips, into
      (90) 1-3/8" x 3-1/2"
      (32) 1-3/8" squares
    (2) 1-3/8" strips, border
    (2) 1-1/8" strips, into
      (64) 1-1/8" squares
Binding
  2" wide scraps

Miniature quilts are always so cute! These little blocks will make you the
star of your quilt group.

Yardage

1/8 yd.	Each, or scraps, of 24 different star fabrics
2/3 yd.	Background
3/4 yd.	Backing

Sewing

1. Make 8 different SnS, Option 1, using a 1-3/4" center square and 1-1/8" star point strip for each.

2. Sew two 1-1/8" background squares to each 1-1/8" outer square as shown below.

Stitch 1-1/8" star point strips to two sides of this unit as shown. Trim, leaving a 1/4" seam allowance on all sides.

3. Sew the stars together using the units from Steps 1 and 2 and the 1-3/8" background squares.

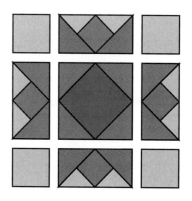

4. Sew the blocks and the 4" background squares into five rows of three, alternating blocks and squares as shown in the diagram.

5. Sew on a 1-3/8" background border according to the border directions on page 8.

6. Sew each of the 1-3/8" colored squares to a 1-3/8" x 3-1/2" background. Stitch 22 of these together for each of the two sides, alternating the colored squares. Stitch 23 together for both the top and the bottom.

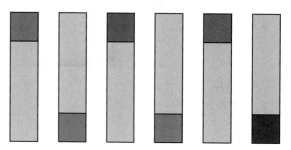

Sew the side borders on, then the top and bottom.

7. Stitch the 2" wide scraps together to make a 2" wide binding.

Desert Star

74" x 86"
Advanced
Photograph, page 24

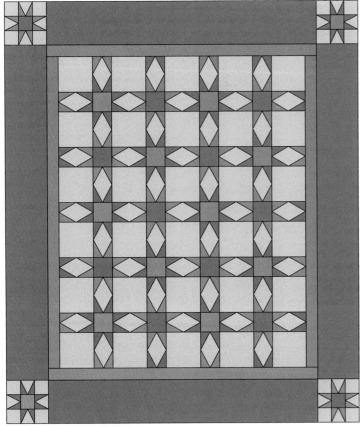

This is the traditional "54 - 40 or Fight" star. I dreamed this quilt during Desert Storm in 1991. Long, thin triangles won't be a nightmare when you use the SnS technique.

Yardage

3-5/8 yds.	Total of 3 or more color A (blue)
2-3/4 yds.	Total of 2 or more color B (red)
3-1/4 yds.	Background
3/4 yd.	Binding
5-1/4 yds.	Backing

Cutting

Color A, assorted
    (7) 6-1/8" strips
    (2) 5-1/8" strips, into
        (10) 5-1/8" squares
        (4) 2-5/8" squares
    (24) 2-1/2" strips
    (2) 1-1/2" strips
Color B, assorted
    (2) 5-1/8" strips, into
        (10) 5-1/8" squares
    (24) 2-1/2" strips
    (7) 2-1/4" strips
    (2) 1-1/2" strips
Background
    (8) 8-1/2" strips, into
        (30) 8-1/2" squares
    (7) 4-1/2" strips
    (1) 2-1/2" strip
    (1) 2-1/4" strip, into
        (16) 2-1/4" squares
Binding
    (8) 3" strips

Sewing

1. Cut the 4-1/2" background strips into (49) 60° diamonds. Lay two strips together, right sides up. Cut a 60° angle along one edge. Cut 4-1/2" segments from this angled edge.

Check the angle after every 3-4 cuts to make sure it remains true; recut if necessary.

2. Sew 49 diamond SnS, Options 7 and 1. Use the 2-1/2" colors A and B strips. Each diamond should have two adjacent color A strips and two adjacent color B strips as shown below.

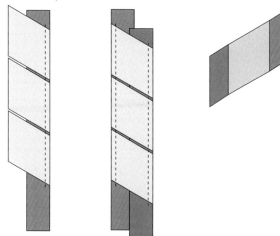

Be sure to leave 1/4" seam allowances on all four sides when cutting. Take care not to stretch the diamonds.

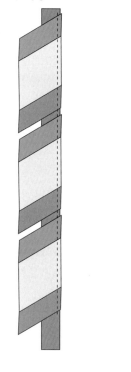

3. Lay the units from Step 2, the 5-1/8" colored squares, and the 8-1/2" background squares out as shown in the quilt diagram. Make sure the color star points and color squares alternate to make stars as shown in the diagram.

Sew in horizontal rows. Stitch the rows together.

4. Sew on the 2-1/4" color B border, following the border instructions, page 8.

5. Make four small stars for the second border. Cut eight 60° diamonds from the 2-1/2" background strip. Cut as explained in Step 1, cutting 2-1/2" segments. Make eight diamond SnS Option 7 and 3, using the 1-1/2" color strips. Make four with color A corner strips and four with color B.

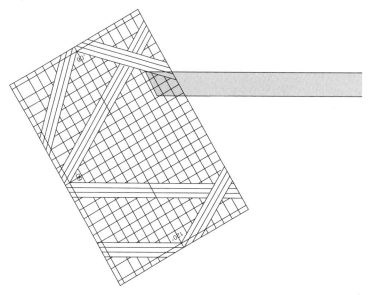

Trim as shown below with 1/4" seam allowances on the sharp points and 1/8" seam allowances on the other points. Cut in half.

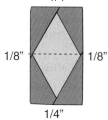

6. Stitch together four stars using the half SnS from Step 5, 2-5/8" color A squares, and 2-1/4" background squares.

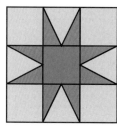

7. Piece 6-1/8" border strips, two the length of the quilt and two the width. Stitch the side borders on. Sew the stars from Step 6 to each end of the remaining borders. Sew these to the top and bottom of the quilt.

Star in Square

16" x 28"
Advanced

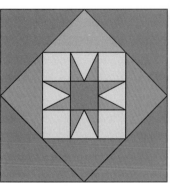

This miniature star in a square is an example of one of the many ways to use the Square in a Square technique. Turn any size block into an SnS, sew them together, add a border, and you're done!

Yardage

3/8 yd.	Color A
1/4 yd.	Color B1 (pieced stars)
1/8 yd.	Color B2 (corner strip)
2/3 yd.	Color B3 (outer corner strips)
1/8 yd.	Star background
1/4 yd.	Binding
5/8 yd.	Backing

Cutting

Color A
   (1) 3-1/4" strip
   (2) 2-3/4" strips
   (2) 1-1/2" strips
Color B1
   (2) 1-1/2" strips
   (2) 2-5/8" squares
Color B2
   (1) 3-1/4" strip
Color B3
   (4) 4-1/2" strips
   (1) 3-1/4" strip

Background
   (1) 2-1/2" strip
Binding
   (3) 2" strips

Sewing

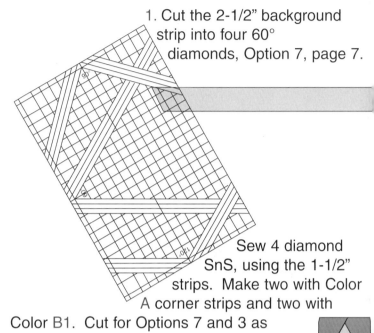

1. Cut the 2-1/2" background strip into four 60° diamonds, Option 7, page 7.

Sew 4 diamond SnS, using the 1-1/2" strips. Make two with Color A corner strips and two with Color B1. Cut for Options 7 and 3 as shown on page 6. The sharp points of the diamond are cut with a 1/4" seam allowance. The other points are cut with a 1/8" seam allowance. Cut in half.

2. Cut the remainder of the 2-1/2" background strip into eight 2-1/4" squares. Stitch together two stars using the half SnS from Step 1, 2-5/8" Color B1 squares, and 2-1/4" background squares.

3. Make 2 SnS, Option 1, using the star blocks as the center square and the various 3-1/4" strips. Sew on a second round, Option 2, using 4-1/2" Color B3 strips.

4. Stitch the blocks together.

5. Add the 2-3/4" Color A border, following the directions on page 8.

Sea of Galilee

14" x 16"
Advanced
Photograph, page 23

Each summer we spend a week at Camp Galilee, a church camp in the Ozarks. This miniature is a memory quilt for me, with each square representing a life change.

Yardage

5/8 yd.	Dark
1/8 yd.	Medium
1/2 yd.	Light
1/8 yd.	Accent (gray)
1/2 yd.	Backing

Cutting

Dark
   (2) 1-1/2" strips
   (7) 1-1/4" strips
   (2) 1" strips
   (2) 2" strips, binding

Medium
   (1) 1-1/2" strip, into
      (9) 1-1/2" squares

Light
   (13) 1-1/4" strips

Accent
   (1) 1-1/4" strip, into
      (8) 1-1/4" squares
      Remainder into 1" strip
   (2) 1" strips

Sewing

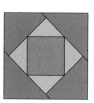

1. Cut (42) 60° diamonds from the 1-1/2" dark strips. Lay the two strips together, right sides up. Cut a 60° angle along one edge. Cut 1-1/2" segments from this angled edge. Check the angle after every 3-4 cuts to make sure it remains true, recutting if necessary.

2. Make 42 SnS, Options 7 and 1. Use the diamonds from Step 1 and 1-1/4" light strips. Be careful not to stretch the diamond when sewing. Leave 1/4" seam allowances when cutting the four points. Use 24 of these in the border.

3. Make 8 SnS, Option 1, using the 1-1/4" accent squares and 1" dark strips.

4. Make 9 SnS Option 2, using 1-1/2" medium squares. The first round is 1" accent strips. The second round is 1-1/4" dark strips.

5. Lay out the units from Steps 2, 3, and 4 as shown in the diagram. Sew into rows. Join the rows.

6. Following the border directions, page 8, sew on a 1-1/4" dark border.

7. Sew the remaining units from Step 2 into four border strips of six units each. Attach to the two long sides of the quilt first. Stitch the other two borders to the top and bottom.

8. Stitch on a 1-1/4" dark border.

Square in a Square™ Technique Ruler
Options 1-7 Instruction Folder included.

Square in a Square™ Book 48 pages. Color pictures. 21 quilt patterns. Highlight options 1-7.

Advancing on With the Square in a Square™ Technique Book
36 pages. New options 8-15 instruc-tions, build-ing from options 1 to 7. Color pictures. 13 quilt patterns using new options. Includes a new tech-nique on quick and easy binding.

Advancing on With the Square in a Square™ Technique Video
Learn quilting the way it was meant to be! This new innovative technique now comes to you in an 89 minute video.

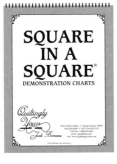

Square in a Square® Demonstration Charts
16 pages. Spiral bound flip chart designed to teach the basic Square in a Square® and Options 1-15

Square in a Square® Teacher's Workbook
104 pages including copy-ready pages for 33 workshops. Works with and compliments the Demonstration Chart.
Includes basics, options, and lesson plans for 32 quilts from the first two books.

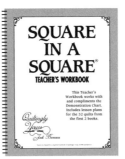

2116 Nevada Dr.
Liberal, Kansas 67901
(316) 624-6260
FAX (316) 624-3115
EMAIL qyjodi@aol.com
WEB www.quiltinglyyours.com

ORDER FORM

QUANTITY

_____ **Square in a Square™ Technique Ruler**
#QYSNS-R1, $19.95 ea.

_____ **Square in a Square™ Book**
#QYSNS-B1, $16.95 ea.

_____ **Advancing on With The Square in a Square™ Technique Book**
#QYSNS-B2, $16.95 ea.

_____ **Advancing on With The Square in a Square™ Technique Video**
#QYSNS-V1, $19.95 ea.

_____ **Square in a Square™ Demonstration Charts**
#QYSNS-B3, $15.00 ea.

_____ **Square in a Square™ Teacher Workbook**
#QYSNS-B4, $45.00 ea.

_____ **TOTAL ITEMS**

SHIPPING: *$4.95*

TOTAL AMOUNT:_____

❏ Check (Make payable to Quiltingly Yours)
❏ Credit Card: __MasterCard   __Visa

#_____

Expiration Date_____

_____
NAME

_____
ADDRESS

_____
CITY, STATE, ZIP

_____
PHONE

❏ Please send information on Trunk Shows
❏ Please send information on Workshops & Lectures

CALL TO ORDER:
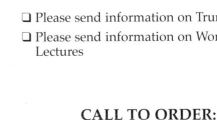
1-888-624-6260
TOLL FREE